# ST DAVI
# CATHEDRAL

D0432998

**Above:**
An aerial view of the cathedral from the north-west, showing the Bishop's Palace and the gatehouse.

**Left:** ③
*Dewi Sant*, David, the patron saint of Wales, portrayed as a bishop in Eucharistic vestments. The dove on his shoulder recalls his eloquence at a 6th-century synod.

## Contents

# History Chart

*c.*589 Death of St David, 1 March.

645–1097 Menevia was ravaged, burnt or destroyed on 13 occasions.

999 Vikings kill Bishop Morgenau.

1080 Vikings kill Bishop Abraham.

1081 William the Conqueror at St Davids. Rhys ap Tewdwr, king of Dyfed, and Gruffydd ap Cynan, king of Gwynedd, meet at Porth Clais.

1089 David's shrine vandalized.

1115 Bernard becomes Bishop.

1131 'Dedication' of church.

1171 and 1172 Henry II visits.

1181–82 Present cathedral begun.

1220 The 'new tower' collapses.

1247 or 1248 Building affected by earthquake.

1328–47 Gower's episcopate: rood screen and Bishop's Palace built.

1365 St Mary's College built.

1509–22 Edward Vaughan's episcopate: Holy Trinity Chapel built.

1530–40 Nave roof and ceiling constructed.

1538 Barlow's letter to Cromwell: destruction of shrine.

1540 Edmund Tudor's tomb was brought to St Davids.

1648 Destruction of building by Parliamentary soldiers.

1793 Nash rebuilds the west front.

1862–77 Sir George Gilbert Scott's restoration.

1901 Lady Chapel restored.

1900–10 The remaining eastern chapels restored.

1982 Queen Elizabeth II distributes the Royal Maundy.

1989–90 Celebration of the 14th centenary of St David's death.

1993 St David's Day celebrations with the Prince of Wales.

1995 Queen Elizabeth II confers city status.

# Dean's Welcome

St Davids is the loveliest of cathedrals to photograph and write about and we are therefore very proud of this guide. We hope that it adds to the richness and enjoyment of your visit, and that, in looking at it later, you will enter once again into the initial experience of this beautiful and holy place. We hope also that others who have not yet visited St Davids will want to do so after seeing this guide.

Having said all that, it is not guides or photography or architecture which come first – these are but adjuncts. Our prime and privileged task is to worship the God who made us and to proclaim Jesus as the Saviour and hope of the world.

May God give you his blessing.

THE DEAN

# Dewi Sant

For over a thousand years, the spot upon which St Davids Cathedral stands has been associated with the patron saint of Wales. It is believed that David founded a monastery here during the 6th century, hence the present Welsh name *Tyddewi* (David's House). Tradition has it that he was also born here, and that Non, his mother, gave birth to him on the spot on the cliffs to the south of the cathedral now marked by the ruins of St Non's Chapel. His baptism was said to have

Below:
The west front of the cathedral by Sir George Gilbert Scott, is a memorial to Connop Thirlwall, Bishop 1840–74.

taken place at Porth Clais, where the River Alun enters the sea, and that a holy well sprang from the ground on the occasion, whose waters healed the blindness of the Irish bishop who baptized him. After being educated by St Paulinus, he came back to *Vetus Rubus* where his uncle had a monastery, before founding his own at a place called *Vallis Rosina*. It was in his own monastery that David died in a year when 1 March fell on a Tuesday, probably 589.

*Vallis Rosina* (*Glyn Rhosyn* in Welsh), 'the valley of the little marsh', is an apt name for the wet valley bottom through which the River Alun flows to the sea. It was on a comparatively dry platform on the bend of the river that the monastic community associated with David placed its church.

The usual medieval name for St Davids was *Menevia* (Welsh *Mynyw*), derived from the Irish *muine*, 'a bush'. It vividly suggests the original state of the valley, dense with bushes and trees, before it was settled by a monastic community. It also reminds us of the deserted and waste places in which David and his contemporaries in the 'Age of the Saints' sought the solitude in which to pursue lives devoted to God.

David stood out even among these heroic figures, the monastic founders of the Celtic West. He expected his monks to spend their time not only in prayer and study but also in hard manual labour. As the 11th-century 'Life of David' has it, 'they place the yoke on their own shoulders' (rather than using oxen to plough the fields); 'they dig into the ground with mattocks and spades, they provide with their own labour all the necessities of the community.' They wore animal skins, had no possessions of their own, and lived on a diet of 'bread and herbs seasoned with salt'. David himself was even more ascetic than his monks, standing for long periods in cold

water to subdue the flesh. It may have been this practice which led to his being known as 'David the Waterman' (*Dewi Ddyfrwr*), as much as his habit of drinking only water.

The Irish resonances of the name *Menevia* bring to mind the presence in south-west Wales of Irish settlers in the post-Roman period. They also remind us that David's asceticism attracted the Irish so that his name is found in Irish calendars of the 9th century. Further, the peninsula upon which St Davids stands lies at the junction of ancient sea and land routes linking Britain to Ireland and the Continent. This proximity to the western seaways brought pilgrims in large numbers to this spot, attracted by the asceticism, learning and devotion which characterized David and his community, and which was the foundation of his reputation for sanctity.

Nor was it among the Irish alone that David's fame had penetrated. In the 9th century, King Alfred summoned Asser from St Davids to help in the rebuilding of intellectual life in Wessex. He went on condition that St Davids gained protection against the Welsh kings who had ravaged it. It was not Welsh kings alone that threatened the community at St Davids, but a more powerful enemy.

# Vikings and Normans

In the 10th and 11th centuries the Vikings, using the western seaways, made frequent raids on the cathedral. Two such raids led to the death of Bishop Morgenau in 999 and Bishop Abraham in 1080. An 11th-century visitor found the saint's shrine hidden in the undergrowth, and the site itself abandoned. It is not surprising that no building earlier than the 12th century survives at St Davids. All that remains from the pre-Norman period are a few inscribed stones such as the Abraham stone now built into the south transept wall.

A descendant of the Norsemen paid a more peaceable visit to St Davids in 1081. William the Conqueror journeyed hither to say his prayers. He may also have had strategic intentions in coming to St Davids, because of its proximity to Ireland. It was not, however, in military terms alone that the Normans posed a threat. They viewed the Welsh church as in dire need of reform. This hostility may have spurred Rhigyfarch, the son of Bishop Sulien, to write a Latin 'Life of David' c.1090, emphasizing the sanctity and orthodoxy of the patron saint. According to Rhigyfarch, David had visited Jerusalem where the patriarch consecrated him bishop. With the coming of the Normans, however, the achievements and independence of the Welsh church were swept away.

In 1115, King Henry I appointed the first Norman Bishop of St Davids, Bernard, who reorganized the diocese on territorial lines. He retained St Davids as the centre of his see and revived a claim that Menevia was the seat of an archbishopric. He transformed the community of clerks (*claswyr*) at St Davids into a chapter of canons, as in any contemporary secular cathedral. Bernard secured a 'privilege' from Pope Calixtus II in 1123, which was tantamount to a canonization of David and was probably instrumental in making St Davids a major centre for pilgrimage throughout the Middle Ages. As the medieval Latin rhyme had it: *Roma semel quantum: bis dat Menevia tantum* (Once to Rome is equal to twice to St Davids). In order to provide a fitting setting for the cult of David, Bernard 'dedicated' a new cathedral in 1131, although he failed to discover St David's body. It is known that in 1089 the shrine had been taken from the church and despoiled of the precious metals which adorned it. Bernard's cathedral has left no trace, except perhaps for some stones in the inner face of the tower, but it was his building which Henry II visited in 1171 and 1172.

# Origins of the Present Cathedral

In 1181 or 1182, the St Davids chronicle tells us that Peter de Leia, Bishop 1176–98, began to rebuild the cathedral. The responsibility for the building works appears to have been shared between Bishop Peter and Giraldus de Barri.

Author, former royal chaplain, ambitious churchman and keen reformer, descended from Norman lords and Welsh princes, Giraldus de Barri or *Giraldus Cambrensis* (Gerald the Welshman), was a canon of St Davids and Archdeacon of Brecon. In 1188, he went around Wales with Baldwin, Archbishop of Canterbury to gather recruits for the Third Crusade. Bishop Peter and Gerald were excused from going on crusade, provided they oversaw the construction of the new cathedral. On the death of Peter de Leia, Giraldus was a candidate for the bishopric. The qualities which seemed eminently to suit him for this task – his undoubted intellectual and organizational abilities and his family connections – were precisely the ones which Henry II and Hubert Walter, the Archbishop of Canterbury, feared in an active Welsh bishop. This and his insistence on the former metropolitan status of St Davids, and its independence from Canterbury, led to his failure although he had taken his cause to Rome. Giraldus retired to Lincoln, where he died *c*.1227, and it is thus unlikely that he was buried at St Davids. It took eight centuries for his vision of an independent church in Wales with its own archbishop to be realized when in 1920 the Church in Wales was disestablished.

The disputed succession to the bishopric did not hold up the building work. The new cathedral had an aisled nave, transepts, a low tower over the crossing, and an aisled presbytery terminating in a flat east end. This plan can still be traced in the present cathedral. It was built in a Transitional Norman style as the combination of round-headed arches

Right: ⑪
This modern statue of Giraldus de Barri (Giraldus Cambrensis, 1146–1227) is set in a Perpendicular niche in Holy Trinity Chapel. His failure to be elected bishop is reflected in the mitre at his feet and not on his head.

Right:
The tower lantern ceiling. The dark colours are medieval; the lighter colours and the episcopal coats of arms date from Scott's restoration. The 14th-century lantern windows and Scott's tie rods can also be seen.

Below:
A nave roof pendant, showing a blend of medieval and Renaissance elements.

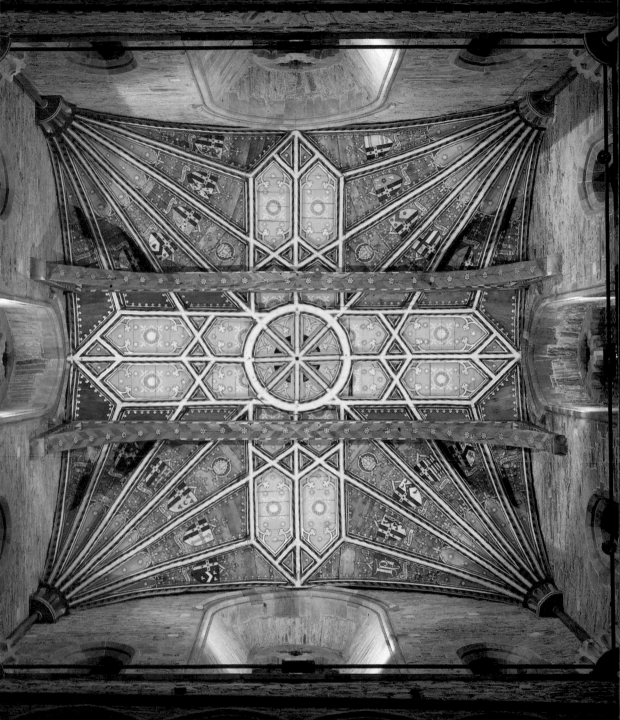

in the nave arcades (Norman/Romanesque) and pointed (Gothic/Early English) arches in the triforium clearly demonstrates.

The 12th-century cathedral probably had a wooden ceiling rather than a stone vault. The inadequacy of the arcade foundations, revealed by their outward

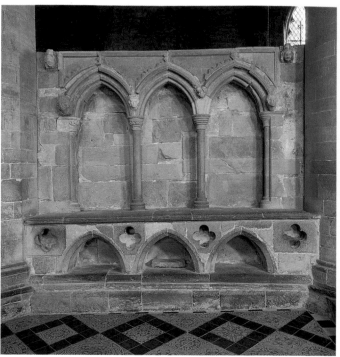

lean, and the thinness of the wall above the triforium made the use of stone impossible. In 1220 the new tower collapsed. In the repair, the western arch was retained, while the other arches were rebuilt in the pointed style, but using the same purple Cambrian sandstone quarried from the cliffs to the south of the cathedral. At this period, west of England oolite was used both in the interior of the tower and in the triple lancets above the high altar. In the same century, the arcades of the presbytery were altered, perhaps as a consequence of earthquake damage, in 1247 or 1248.

Its Early English piscina dates the original building of the Chapel of St Thomas Becket to the early 13th century. It was perhaps built as a consequence of Henry II's visit. At the end of the same century, a Lady Chapel was built to the east of the main cathedral building opening off an earlier ambu-

latory. This covered walkway appears to be connected with the cult of St David.

In 1275, a new shrine was built on the north side of the presbytery; its ruined base is still in position today. It was placed there for easier access by pilgrims, replacing an earlier structure near the niche under the central eastern lancet, which belongs to the first building phase of the present cathedral. The 'rediscovery' of David's body may well be related to the transfer of the shrine to its new position. It was at this new shrine that Edward I prayed in 1284.

The last decades of the 13th century also saw the construction of one of the dominant features of the cathedral close. The bell tower against which the one surviving medieval gateway was built, and from which it takes its name, Porth y Twr, was built on the edge of the valley in order to enable the sound of the bells to carry over a greater distance.

**Above:** ⑭
St David's shrine, built in 1275 and destroyed at the Reformation. This is the stone base upon which the relics of David and Justinian were kept in a portable casket, or feretory. It was once surmounted by an ornamental wooden canopy and murals of David, Patrick and Denis of France filled the arches.

**Above left:** ⑪
Detail of the Perpendicular fan-vaulting of the ceiling of Holy Trinity Chapel. The coats of arms are those of Henry VII (nearer camera) and Edward Vaughan, impaling those of the diocese.

In the middle of the 14th century, the cathedral and its precincts were transformed, probably under the direction of Bishop Henry Gower. A wall was constructed, to enclose the houses of the cathedral Chapter as well as to separate the city from the secular world outside. It may also have been defensive in intent since portions of it retain battlements. The wall was pierced by four gates: *Porth Padrig* (Patrick's Gate), below the present deanery; *Porth Gwyn* (the White Gate) above the Bishop's Palace; *Porth Bonyng* (Bonyng's Gate) at the north east end of the close; and *Porth y Tŵr* (The Gate of the Tower). Besides this last, the only remainder of the gates is a single jamb of Porth Bonyng.

**Above:**
The only surviving gateway into the close is Porth y Tŵr. The gateway is built against the 13th-century octagonal tower in which the cathedral bells are hung.

**Left:** ⑤
The buttress supporting the eastern arch of the tower is part of the archway into the presbytery from the south transept. The presbytery vaulting shafts, as is clear from the picture, never fulfilled their intended function of holding up a stone-vaulted roof. The floor tiles are Victorian.

11

Bishop Gower's epitaph in the cathedral rightly attributes the building of the Bishop's Palace to him. Although parts are earlier, he gave the palace its present distinctive appearance. The east range contained the episcopal apartments whereas the south range with its great hall, parlour and chapel were designed for the entertainment of distinguished pilgrims. Gower harmonized the disparate parts of the palace by constructing a remarkable arched parapet walk in the Decorated style.

In the cathedral, Gower undertook a major remodelling in the Decorated style. He heightened the aisles of the nave, presbytery and choir, inserted new and larger windows, and added the middle or lantern stage to the tower. He also added the sedilia and tombs to the Lady Chapel. The south door of the nave was enlarged and a two-storey stone vaulted porch constructed to protect it. He completely remodelled St Thomas's Chapel as a three-storey building with the Chapter House and treasury above. The stone-vaulted ceiling of the chapel with its fine carved bosses is matched by the window seat and fireplace of the Chapter House (the present library) as testimony to the abilities of Gower's masons.

The finest expression of their art, however, is the stone screen or pulpitum which divides the nave from the choir, replacing an earlier screen blocking the western arch of the tower. Gower's pulpitum appears to have absorbed at least part of this. Both within the tomb space on the north side and on the screen as a whole there are traces of bright polychrome decoration.

The skeleton vaulting in the screen passage, together with a star-shaped tomb canopy in the south nave aisle are reminiscent of contemporary work in Bristol Cathedral. The southern compartment of the screen contains Gower's

own tomb and, although battered, it is a fitting memorial to an able and energetic medieval bishop who had served both church and state; as indeed is the bishop's throne which also appears to have been constructed during Gower's episcopate.

Following the death of Gower in 1347, no further large-scale building projects appear to have been undertaken at St Davids, with the exception of the College of the Blessed Virgin Mary in 1365. Its builder, Bishop Adam Houghton, although born near St Davids, had been a royal civil servant, which may account for the association of John of Gaunt and his wife Blanche as patrons of the college. Houghton founded the college for a master and seven fellows to ensure the proper maintenance of the divine offices. All that remains is the former chapel on the north side of the cathedral now converted as the cathedral hall, although the modern house known as Cloister Hall and its garden are built over the basement of the collegiate buildings. At the same period, a cloister connecting the college with the cathedral was begun, but never completed.

External and internal splendour. The cathedral from the west, viewed across the Bishop's Palace, and, inset, the wooden crucifix which hangs from the nave ceiling above the pulpitum, a fine 20th-century replacement for the destroyed medieval rood. Even in ruin, Henry Gower's Bishop's Palace surprises by the quality of its architecture. The wheel window in the east gable of the great hall and the arcading on top of the walls are clearly visible.

**Left:** (14)
The presbytery looking east from the organ loft. The beams supporting the roof were renewed during 19th-century restoration. The mosaics in the lancets by Salviati date also from the 19th century. The tomb before the altar is that of Edmund Tudor, Earl of Richmond.

In the 15th and 16th centuries, major restoration and reconstruction were undertaken on the cathedral. The side walls of the presbytery were raised, a flat painted camber-beam roof inserted and a new large single window replaced the upper series of lancets. At ground level, the sanctuary was relaid with encaustic tiles, which can still be seen, and a new set of choir stalls was constructed. These survive in excellent condition and are distinguished both by the carving on the misericords and by the traces of colouring on the backs of the stalls. The Prince of Wales's feathers and pomegranates carved on two poppy heads, the coats of arms on the backs of the stalls and on bench ends, the patterns of the floor tiles in the sanctuary, the painted ceilings of the tower lantern and the presbytery, the fine wooden sedilia surviving on the south side of the sanctuary all seem to suggest a date in the late 15th or early 16th centuries. The rearrangement of the parclose screen and the throne are associated with the episcopate of John Morgan (1496–1504) whose coat of arms was once painted on the back of the throne and who lies buried in a tomb decorated with carvings in the Renais-sance style on the south side of the nave.

No doubt as to date or style attaches to Holy Trinity Chapel. Here, in what had been an open courtyard blocked with rubbish, Edward Vaughan, Bishop 1509–22, constructed a chantry chapel dedicated to the Holy Trinity, in which he lies buried. This exquisite chapel, lined with oolitic limestone, was built in a restrained version of the Perpendicular style, complete with fan vaulting. The unknown architect adorned the roof and walls with fine carving and provided window openings, later blocked, which allowed the chantry priest celebrating at the altar of the Holy Trinity to follow the progress of masses in the Lady Chapel and the Chapels of St Nicholas and St Edward the Confessor. Unfortunately, the construction of the chapel necessitated the blocking of the triple lancets over the high altar and it may have been at this period that the niche beneath the lancets was blocked.

Further east, Vaughan remodelled the Lady Chapel as a two-bay structure with vaulted roof, as well as rebuilding and heightening the antechapel. He was also responsible for adding the upper stage to the tower.

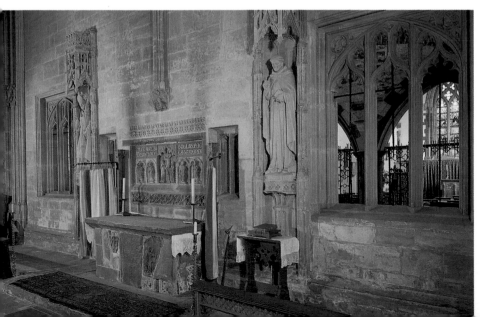

**Left:** (11)
Holy Trinity Chapel, constructed in the Perpendicular style by Bishop Edward Vaughan (1509–22) as his chantry chapel. A modern statue of Vaughan is in one niche; in the other, one of Giraldus Cambrensis (1146–1227). Altar and altarpiece are reconstructions from medieval fragments.

There was, however, one major piece of reconstruction that became necessary during this period of the cathedral's history. Whereas the changes which affected the east end of the building followed from a general desire to reorder and reorganize, the work which was undertaken on the nave was the result of the inadequacy of the 12th-century

foundations. The outward lean of the north nave arcade led to the provision of massive external props to the aisle wall and flying buttresses to the arcade. The roof of the nave was lowered and concealed by an oak ceiling, suspended from the tie beams. The flatness of the ceiling is disguised by the arches and pendants which so profusely enrich it. The decoration on this *tour de force* of the carpenter's art draws on both late medieval motifs like the 'Green Man', also visible on the misericords, and Renaissance features such as the dragon-shaped dolphins which adorn most of the pendants. By a happy coincidence, an expedient to counteract disaster has become one of the glories of the cathedral. Traditionally ascribed to the late 15th century, the presence of Renaissance motifs and the evidence of contemporary documents show that the ceiling was probably still unfinished as late as 1538.

Above:
The nave looking west. The arcade consists of alternate round and octagonal piers, carrying wide arches. The triforium is a light stone screen contained within the clerestory. The stained glass in the west window is modern.

Left: ⑫
The sedilia, seating for the priest, deacon and sub-deacon celebrating mass at the high altar. Of medieval date and in the Perpendicular style, this fine example is a rare survival. The base and seat backings are of modern origin.

**Right:**
The Lady Chapel.
Roofless for almost
two centuries, the
Chapel of the Blessed
Virgin Mary was
restored in 1901.
Many of the bosses in
the roof are medieval.
The sedilia and tombs,
much restored, date
from Bishop Gower's
episcopate.

# The Reformation

**Right:** ⑭
The brass on the tomb
of Edmund Tudor, Earl
of Richmond and
father of Henry VII, is a
fine Victorian replica
replacing the original
which was torn away
in the 17th century.
The feet rest on a
greyhound, one of the
supporters of the
Tudor coat of arms.

The tide of ecclesiastical reform reached St Davids in the person of William Barlow, Bishop 1536–48. Barlow was a Protestant of strong convictions and under the patronage first of Queen Anne Boleyn, then of Thomas Cromwell. In order to break the hold of what he saw as 'superstition', he not only urged the removal of the cathedral to the centre of the diocese at Carmarthen but slighted the shrine of David, stripped it of its jewels and confiscated the relics of David and Justinian. Apart from the attack on the relics, the cathedral seems to have suffered very little material damage at this stage of the Reformation. Indeed, it gained in that the tomb of Edmund Tudor, Earl of Richmond and Henry VII's father, was transferred to its present position before the high altar on the dissolution of the Greyfriars at Carmarthen. The Bishop's Palace was not so fortunate. Hostile St Davids gossip blamed Barlow for stripping the lead from the roof in order to provide dowries for his six daughters. Given that his daughters were not born when he was at St Davids, this seems unlikely. And in any case, the domestic apartments of the bishops appear to have remained in use until the mid 17th century.

# Iconoclasm and Destruction

**Left:** ⑪
The original pilgrim's recess in Holy Trinity Chapel set in the former 12th-century external wall. Above are the triple lancets blocked when the chapel was built. Medieval bones long believed to be those of David and Justinian are contained in the oak casket.

The later 16th century saw the dissolution of St Mary's College in 1549, the end of communal life for the College of Vicars Choral (the clerics appointed by the Chapter to maintain the round of services) and the destruction of the chantries within the cathedral. In the light of the changes wrought by the Reformation it is not surprising that the remaining medieval service books were destroyed as remnants of the old order: in 1550 by Bishop Ferrar, who was burnt at the stake in 1554; and in 1571, when the rood loft was removed and the pulpit constructed, by Thomas Huett, the Precentor, who with Richard Davies, Bishop 1561–81, was one of the translators of the Welsh New Testament of 1567. Far more damage was done, however, by Parliamentary soldiers who were dispatched to get lead from the roof in 1648. They wrecked what remained of the medieval library, destroyed the organ and bells, smashed stained glass and tore up tomb brasses. As a consequence, the east end of the cathedral, stripped of its lead, fell into decay and remained unroofed for over two centuries. With very slender financial resources, however, the canons of the Restoration period and the early 18th century, succeeded in regaining the use of the presbytery and transepts by walling up the arches of the former and releading the roofs of the latter.

**Right:** ⑮
The royal stall. Uniquely, the sovereign of the United Kingdom is a member of the Chapter, as a result, perhaps, of the dissolution of St Mary's College. The only sovereign to have occupied this First Cursal stall is Queen Elizabeth II.

# Restoration: Nash, Butterfield and Scott

By the end of the 18th century, concern was increasingly being expressed about the condition of the west front of the cathedral. The 16th-century repairs to the nave had not solved the problems of the sloping and waterlogged site, since the west front had not only moved almost three feet out of the perpendicular, but was continuing to move at the rate of half an inch a year and was tearing the nave piers apart at the same time. The well-known architect John Nash was engaged in 1793 by the Chapter to put matters right. The design which he adopted was a mixture of Gothic styles, vaguely Perpendicular, which indeed contained real Perpendicular work since he vandalized the windows of St Mary's College chapel and used their tracery in the west front. A little earlier than this, Nash had constructed a new Chapter House near the south gate but this, like his work on the cathedral, was not destined to last. The former disappeared within fifty years,

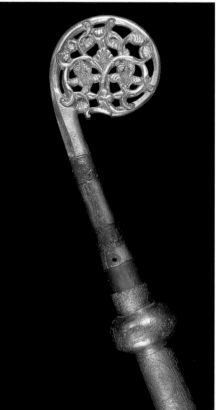

**Above:**
This view published by the brothers Buck in 1740 shows the ruinous condition into which the east end of the cathedral had sunk by the 18th century. In most respects, however, the cathedral and its environs are unchanged.

**Left:** ⑰
Among the treasures of the cathedral is this crozier head recovered from the grave reputed to be that of Bishop Richard de Carew (d.1280). His tomb was disturbed during Scott's restoration. The crozier, of gilt bronze with niello decoration, dates from c.1150.

leaving only the traces of its foundations, and the latter vanished within a century, victim not only to the weathering of the soft stone but to changing architectural taste and the more thoroughgoing restoration which followed.

During the first half of the 19th century, further restoration and improvement work had to be undertaken. William Butterfield repaired the tiles of the dais before the pulpitum, placed new windows in the nave aisles, inserted the large Perpendicular-style window in the north transept and in 1844 transformed the south transept into a parish church. These works had, however, not dealt with the most serious problems facing the building.

In 1862, Sir George Gilbert Scott, having been commissioned to survey the cathedral, reported on the parlous state of the building, drawing particular

attention to the condition of the tower, which was in imminent danger of collapse. Thus began the work which within a century saw the complete restoration and refurbishment of the cathedral. Scott began with the tower. It is clear from the provision of blocking walls in three of the main arches that the stability of the tower had caused concern from the medieval period onwards, not least because of the addition of two stages to the original 12th-century structure. This had itself been damaged by earthquake and collapse. The weight of seven heavy bells – one of which can still be seen at the back of the nave – had not aided matters nor had the damage wrought by the removal of the same bells in the 17th century. The basic fault, however, was both with the foundations and with the sloping site, which had led Scott to realize that the only support received by the badly crushed western piers of the tower came from the transept walls and the nave arcades. It was probably the westward movement of the tower which had, at least in part, caused both the distortion of the nave arcades and the outward lean of the west front. Scott's achievement was remarkable in that he succeeded in rebuilding the tower without taking it down, as well as providing foundations for it.

At the same time the presbytery was sensitively refurbished and the 15th-century roof restored and repainted. Scott had at first intended to replace the flat roof with one more in keeping with the 13th-century original. But for his sensitivity to the building history of the cathedral and the availability of suitable oak to replace the decayed camber beams, he would have created a steeply-pitched roof similar to that in both transepts. Scott's work at St Davids was generally sympathetic to the building history and traditions of the cathedral. Mosaics by Salviati were inserted into

the triplet; the large Perpendicular window above was removed, the form of the original quadruplet was recovered and the lights glazed with glass by Hardman; a new brass was placed on the tomb of Edward Tudor; and the tiles of the presbytery floor, with the exception of those within the altar rails, were replaced.

The nave and transepts were also restored, the whole culminating in the replacement of the west front by a design more in keeping with the Transitional style of the original west front, but with the upper range of windows round-headed and not pointed. The front itself was planned as a memorial to Connop Thirlwall, the distinguished scholar who was Bishop of St Davids 1840–74, and largely instrumental in beginning the restoration work.

Above: (8)
The Chapel of St Edward the Confessor. The tomb is that of the Countess of Maidstone, granddaughter of Bishop Jenkinson (1825–40). His robes for the 1837 Coronation are in the showcase on the left.

**Left:** ⑮
The pair of trumpeting angels which surmount the projecting organ parapet are a happy modern addition to the choir furnishings.

**Below:** ①
The destruction of stained glass by Parliamentary soldiers is a matter for regret. Fortunately the cathedral gained in the 1950s by the insertion of glass by the William Morris studios as in this example above the font at the west end of the nave.

After Scott's death, his son Oldrid oversaw the restoration of the Lady Chapel to its Perpendicular form in 1901, using much medieval material especially as regards the roof bosses. Under successive generations of the Caroe family, the whole of the cathedral has been reroofed and brought back into use. The last chapel to be reroofed was that of St Edward the Confessor which now contains an altar tomb and fittings in alabaster as a memorial to the Countess of Maidstone, who paid for the restoration of the south chapel aisle in which St Edward's Chapel lies.

It was during this early 20th-century phase of restoration (1920), that the niche in Holy Trinity Chapel, first opened out by Scott, was fitted up with an oak reliquary and grille. Bones first discovered in 1866 sealed up in the recess and then buried under the floor of the chapel, were placed within the oak casket. It was long believed that they may be some of the bones of David and Justinian, placed here for safe-keeping following the destruction of the shrine in 1538. The 20th century has also seen the placing of a new hanging rood above the pulpitum in the nave, the replacement and refurbishment of the nave furniture, the countering of the ravages of the deathwatch beetle, the refurbishment of St Thomas Becket's Chapel (the Blessed Sacrament is reserved in it) and the transformation of the former Chapter House and treasury into the cathedral library. The Willis organ, which incorporates an earlier one by Schmidt, received its new case, and has twice been rebuilt; the heating and lighting systems have been replaced and new sound systems installed. Outside the cathedral, Porth y Twr received a ring of bells in 1931 and the chapel of St Mary's College became the cathedral hall in 1966. In 1993 a new choir room was built between two of the cloister buttresses.

# The Cathedral Today

Anyone visiting St Davids in high summer finds the cathedral thronged with people, many of whom have come to view the architecture and savour the atmosphere of an historic building. The cathedral does not, however, fall silent during the rest of the year. For this is no museum, but a church serving a living community. That community of faith extends far beyond St Davids itself. It includes those who maintain the *Opus Dei*, the daily round of ordered worship begun by David's own community as they sought to establish a place of order and quiet among the insecurities of their time. It also includes those who welcome all who come to the cathedral and those whose handiwork keeps the building adorned and in repair. It embraces those who worship here Sunday by Sunday, for the cathedral is also the parish church of St Davids. Here generations

**Left:** (15)
Two examples of the carvings which grace the underside of the tip-up misericord seats. Above *Two Dancers* and below *Seasickness* express the wit and irony of the 16th-century craftsmen.

**Above:** (15)
A detail from the choir stalls carved in the late 15th or early 16th century.

**Left:**
The Chapter badge. The unique association between the sovereign and St Davids is embodied in the design of the badge worn by members of the cathedral Chapter.

**Far left:** (15)
The Bishop's throne was moved to its present position on the south side of the choir in the early 16th century when the present parclose was displaced to accommodate it. Traces of painted figures can still be seen on parts of the throne's spire.

**Above:**     ⑮
Directly beneath the
tower and behind the
organ lies the choir. The
present stalls date from
the late 15th or early
16th century. Unusually
the Bishop has a stall on
the south side in what
was normally the Dean's
place.

have made their communion, been baptized in the font, married at the altar and buried in the precincts.

Again, this community is represented by the people who live in the diocese of St Davids, who look to the cathedral as their mother church and who come here regularly on great occasions to give thanks for the life of the diocese and to pray for its clergy and people. Each year many organisations and institutions, local and national, come to St Davids Cathedral to celebrate important events in their calendar. Above all, the community which St Davids Cathedral exists to serve is represented by those who are prepared to make their journey to the far west of Wales to say their prayers and find peace on a spot which has been sanctified by prayer and devotion for over a thousand years.

**Top:**
The nave choir stalls with a Sunday service taking place.

**Left:**
A service in progress. The cathedral is not only the mother church of the diocese, but also the parish church of the city of St Davids.

**Above:**
A memorable feature of the cathedral is due to the service of the volunteers who provide the flowers. These adorn and complement both the detail of the architecture and the colour of the stone, as here before the statue of the patron saint.